SUPERSTARS OF WRESTLING

DANIEL BRYAN

BY BENJAMIN PROUDFIT

HOT TOPICS

Gareth Stevens
PUBLISHING

Please visit our website, www.garethstevens.com. For a free color catalog of all our high-quality books, call toll free 1-800-542-2595 or fax 1-877-542-2596.

Library of Congress Cataloging-in-Publication Data

Names: Proudfit, Benjamin, author.
Title: Daniel Bryan / Benjamin Proudfit.
Description: New York : Gareth Stevens Publishing, 2019. | Series: Superstars of wrestling | Includes index.
Identifiers: LCCN 2017050100| ISBN 9781538221037 (library bound) | ISBN 9781538221051 (pbk.) | ISBN 9781538221068 (6 pack)
Subjects: LCSH: Bryan, Daniel, 1981---Juvenile literature. | Wrestlers--United States--Biography--Juvenile literature.
Classification: LCC GV1196.B79 P76 2019 | DDC 796.812092 [B] --dc23 LC record available at https://lccn.loc.gov/2017050100

First Edition

Published in 2019 by
Gareth Stevens Publishing
111 East 14th Street, Suite 349
New York, NY 10003

Designer: Sarah Liddell
Editor: Kristen Nelson

Photo credits: Cover, p. 1 Chris Ryan/Contributor/Corbis Sport/Getty Images; pp. 5, 21 FlickrWarrior/Wikimedia Commons; p. 7 Chris Ryan - Corbis/Contributor/Corbis Sport/Getty Images; p. 9 Gallo Images/Stringer/Getty Images Sport/Getty Images; pp. 11, 19 Icon Sport/Contributor/Icon Sport/Getty Images; p. 13 NiciVampireHeart/Wikimedia Commons; p. 15 Maurilbert/Wikimedia Commons; p. 17 Gallo Images/Stringer/Getty Images Entertainment/Getty Images; p. 23 Shipjustgotreal/Wikimedia Commons; p. 25 Prefall/Wikimedia Commons; p. 27 Starship.paint/Wikimedia Commons; p. 29 Paul Warner/Contributor/Getty Images Entertainment/Getty Images.

Printed in the United States of America

CPSIA compliance information: Batch #CS18GS: For further information contact Gareth Stevens, New York, New York at 1-800-542-2595.

CONTENTS

SMALL BUT TOUGH

Many wrestling fans know Daniel Bryan as the World Wrestling Entertainment (WWE) **underdog**. He's small for a wrestler at 5 feet 8 inches (1.7 m). But Daniel spent years working hard in the ring. He became one of the best wrestlers in the world!

IN THE RING

Daniel was born Bryan Danielson on May 22, 1981. He mostly grew up in Aberdeen, Washington.

LOVE AT FIRST SIGHT

As a kid, Daniel **stuttered** and was sick a lot. He played sports but wasn't great at any of them. Daniel didn't know anything about **professional** wrestling until a friend showed him a wrestling magazine. He started watching it on TV—and got hooked.

IN THE RING

In middle school, Daniel and some friends wrestled a giant teddy bear for fun! They called it Backyard Championship Wrestling.

JUMPING IN

In high school, Daniel knew he wanted to be a professional wrestler. He lied to get out of school in order to train more and work to save money to go to wrestling school. After finishing high school, he moved to San Antonio, Texas.

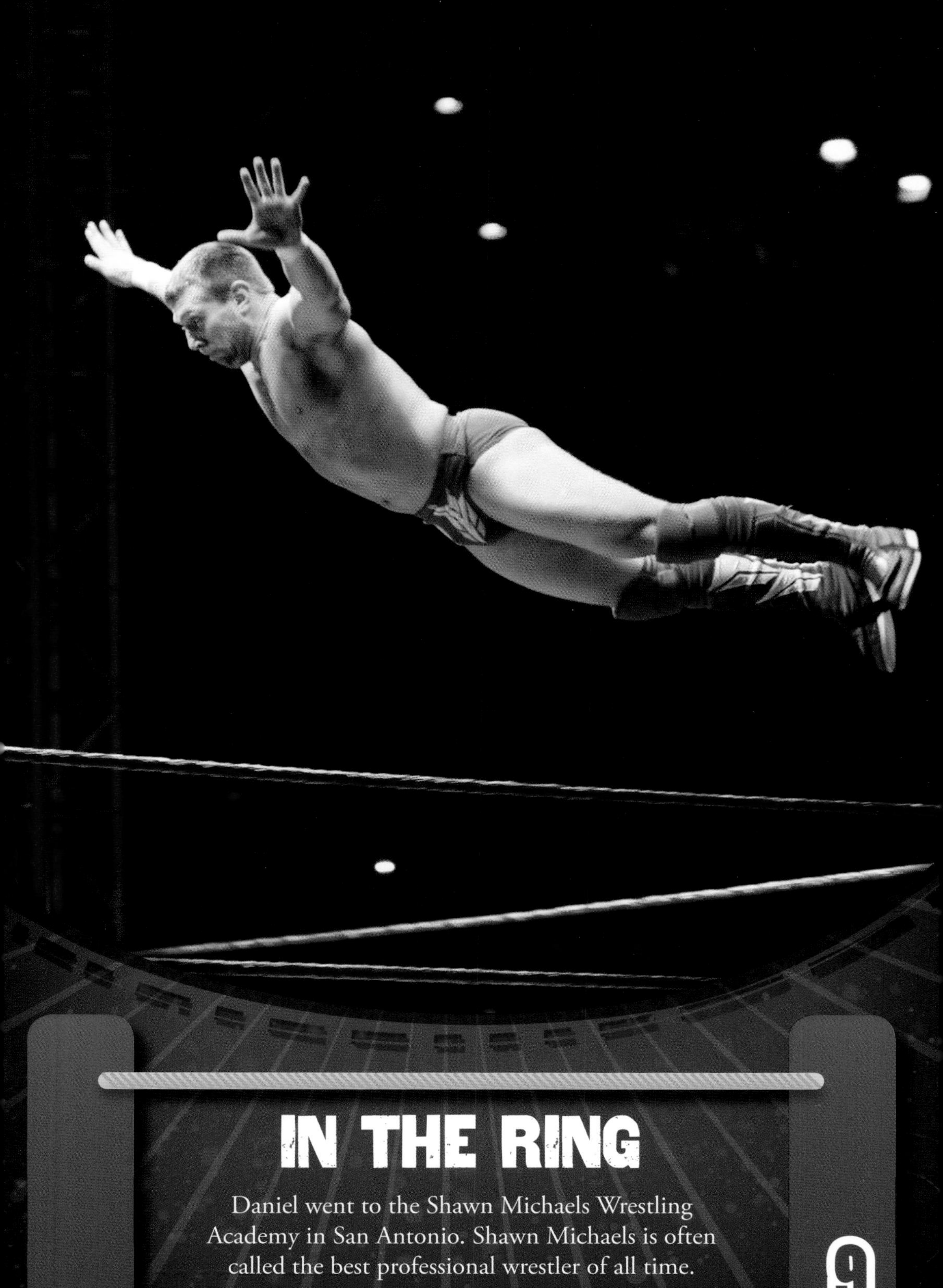

IN THE RING

Daniel went to the Shawn Michaels Wrestling Academy in San Antonio. Shawn Michaels is often called the best professional wrestler of all time.

Daniel had his first professional match as a wrestler just a few months later in October 1999. He wore a mask and went by the name the American Dragon. A few months later, he had a chance to wrestle in Japan for the first time!

IN THE RING

In February 2000, Daniel began working for WWE in Memphis Championship Wrestling (MCW). It didn't last. MCW was shut down, and Daniel was let go in 2001.

IN THE INDIES

In 2001, Daniel won the King of the Indies **tournament**. He started to be noticed by wrestling companies in the United States and around the world. In 2002, Daniel began wrestling many shows with a new company, Ring of Honor (ROH).

IN THE RING

Daniel has wrestled in England, Japan, and Mexico as an independent wrestler. Being independent, or indie, means working on shows smaller than those put on by big companies such as WWE.

ROH CHAMP

In ROH, Daniel was mostly known by his real name, Bryan Danielson. He won the ROH World Championship in September 2005. He held this title for 462 days! At the end of 2006, a hurt shoulder caused him to take time off.

IN THE RING

Daniel got hurt many times as a wrestler, including several **concussions**. These would be an ongoing problem for him.

FALSE START

Daniel started working hard at learning more martial arts, such as kickboxing and jujitsu. By 2009, he was known as one of the best indie wrestlers. His goal that year was to make it to WWE. By October, WWE had signed him!

IN THE RING

Daniel started on WWE's **competition** show *NXT*. Daniel didn't do well on the show, broke a few rules on WWE's *Raw* TV show, and was let go from the company again.

WWE CHAMPION

WWE asked Daniel to come back for SummerSlam in August 2010. By September, he had won the US Championship title. The following July, he won the Money in the Bank **contract**. He cashed it in at TLC in December 2011 and won the World Heavyweight Championship!

IN THE RING

When he first came back to WWE in 2010, Daniel spent time working with the Bella Twins, Brie and Nikki. He and Brie fell in love! They got married in April 2014.

YES!

Daniel had become very popular with fans. His "Yes! Yes! Yes!" chant was often very loud, even when he wasn't in the ring. So when he lost the World Heavyweight Championship in an 18-second match at WrestleMania 28, the fans were angry.

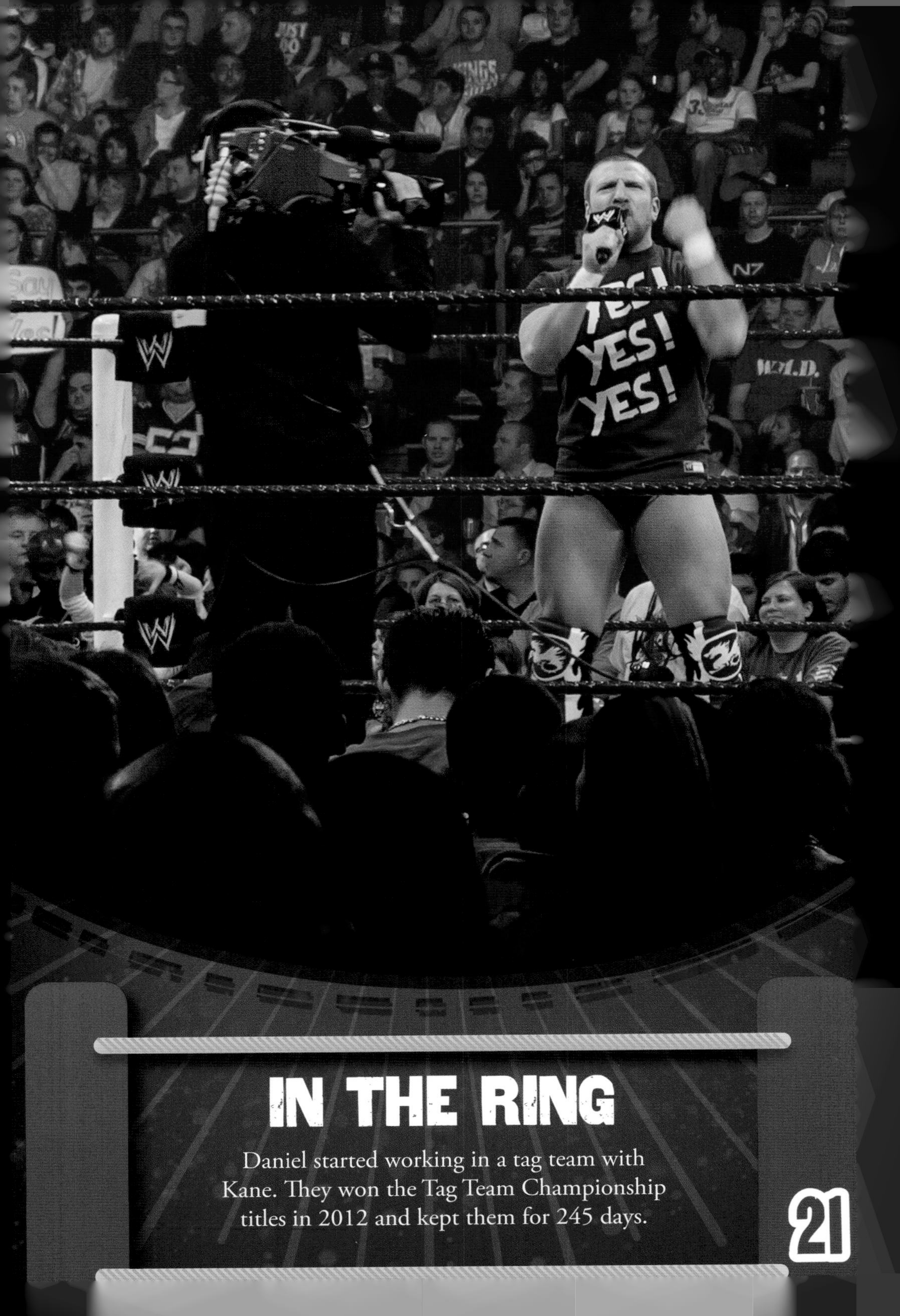

IN THE RING

Daniel started working in a tag team with Kane. They won the Tag Team Championship titles in 2012 and kept them for 245 days.

In 2013, Daniel fell on his neck and shoulder during a match. He wrestled in pain, but won the WWE Championship at SummerSlam. Then, Randy Orton cashed in his Money in the Bank contract and took it from him a few minutes later!

IN THE RING

Daniel won the fan vote for the 2013 Slammy Award for Superstar of the Year!

'MANIA WINS

At the 2014 Royal Rumble, fans booed the final wrestlers because Daniel wasn't one of them. So, he wrestled Triple H at WrestleMania 30. When Daniel won, he was entered into the match for the World Heavyweight Championship later in the night—and won!

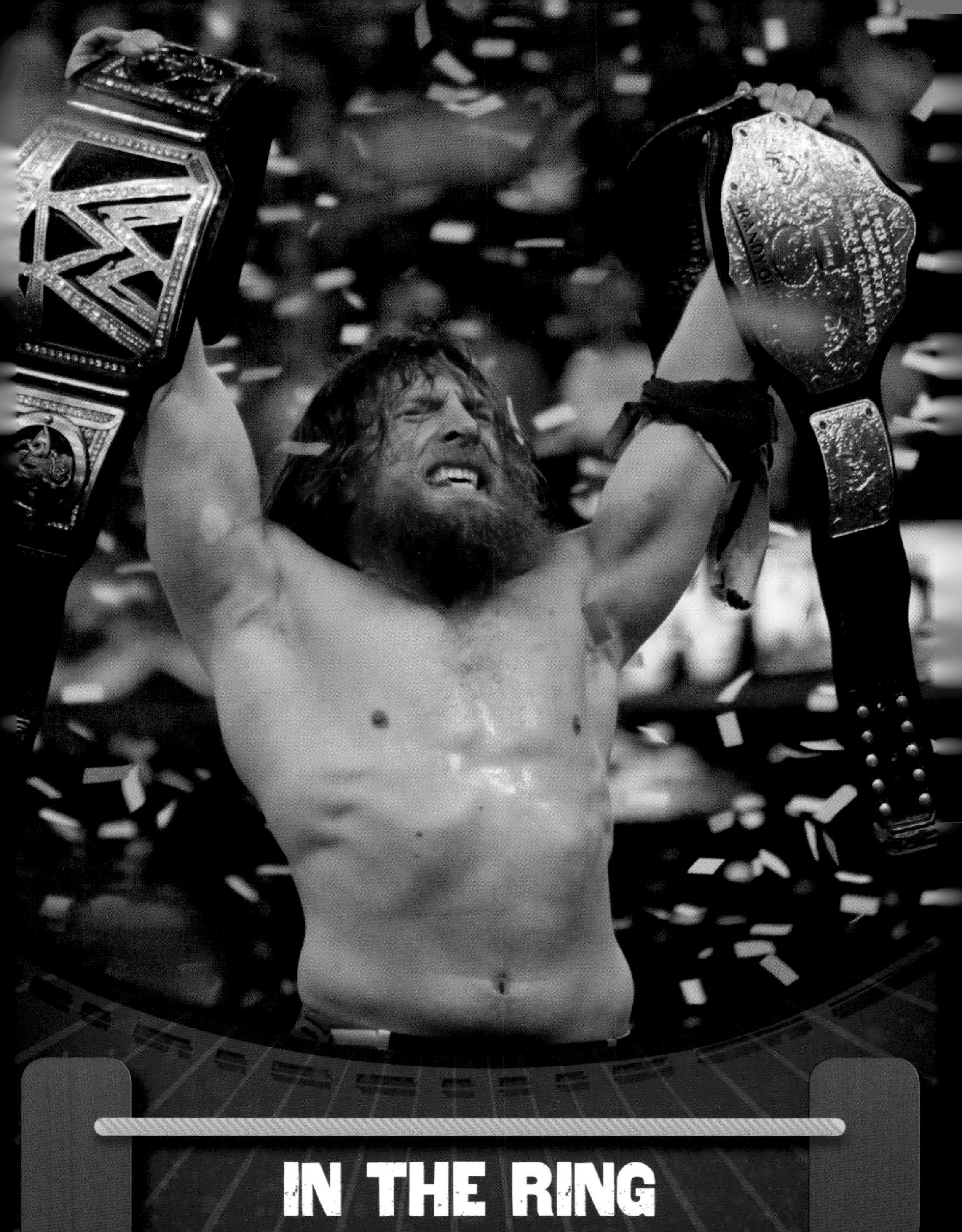

IN THE RING

On May 12, 2014, Daniel announced his neck was hurt badly, and he needed a doctor to fix it. WWE made him give up the championship while he was out that summer.

Daniel healed enough to begin wrestling again in November 2014. He was part of the 2015 Royal Rumble a few months later but was out early. Fans were angry again. But Daniel went on to win the Intercontinental Title at WrestleMania 31!

IN THE RING

Daniel got hurt again and had to give up his title in May 2015. In February 2016, Daniel announced he was **retiring**.

WHAT'S NEXT?

Daniel became the general manager of *SmackDown Live* in July 2016. He believes he will wrestle again, despite the many concussions from his time in the ring. As he said in 2015: "I really don't know life without wrestling."

IN THE RING

A little boy named Connor Michalek was Daniel's biggest fan. Daniel met Connor many times, even though Connor was very sick. Members of WWE started Connor's Cure in 2014 in his honor.

THE BEST OF DANIEL BRYAN

SIGNATURE MOVES

Yes! kicks, front missile drop kick

FINISHER

Yes! lock

ACCOMPLISHMENTS

Ring of Honor Champion;
Grand Slam in WWE (WWE,
World Heavyweight, Tag Team, US,
and Intercontinental championships)

MATCHES TO WATCH

Daniel Bryan vs. Batista vs.
Randy Orton at WrestleMania 30;
Daniel Bryan vs. John Cena
at SummerSlam 2013

FOR MORE INFORMATION

BOOKS

Chandler, Matt. *Outrageous Pro Wrestling Rivalries*. North Mankato, MN: Capstone Press, 2015.

Pantaleo, Steve. *Daniel Bryan*. Indianapolis, IN: DK/BradyGames, 2014.

WEBSITES

Daniel Bryan
www.wwe.com/superstars/daniel-bryan
Visit Daniel Bryan's official WWE page here.

Connor's Cure
www.givetochildrens.org/aboutconnorscure
Learn more about the foundation founded in honor of Daniel's young friend and fan Connor.

GLOSSARY

competition: an event in which people try to win

concussion: an injury to the brain caused by someone hitting their head hard

contract: a written agreement between two parties

professional: earning money from an activity that many people do for fun

retire: to leave a job

stutter: to repeat the first sounds of some words

tournament: a series of contests testing the skill of many athletes in the same sport

underdog: a person or team expected to lose a contest

INDEX